TEEN MENTAL HEALTH™

anxiety and
panic attacks

Judith Levin

ROSEN
PUBLISHING®
New York

Published in 2009 by The Rosen Publishing Group, Inc.
29 East 21st Street, New York, NY 10010

Copyright © 2009 by The Rosen Publishing Group, Inc.

First Edition

Library of Congress Cataloging-in-Publication Data

Levin, Judith (Judith N.), 1956–
Anxiety and panic attacks / Judith Levin.
    p. cm.—(Teen mental health)
Includes bibliographical references and index.
ISBN-13: 978-1-4042-1797-3 (library binding)
1. Anxiety disorders—Juvenile literature. 2. Panic attacks—Juvenile literature. I. Title.
RC531.L39 2008
616.85'22—dc22

                                  2008007144

Manufactured in the United States of America

CPSIA Compliance Information: Batch #BR013080YA: For further information, contact Rosen Publishing, New York, New York, at 1-800-237-9932.

contents

chapter one

What Are Anxiety and Panic Attacks?

Everybody feels anxiety sometimes. It is normal to worry about big exams, first dates, or what might happen if your parents keep fighting. There are actually positive benefits of stress, including motivating a person to take action, but anxiety can become so overwhelming that it interferes with day-to-day living. As Laura Melano Flanagan, a therapist in New York City, puts it, "It's about something dreadful that might happen outside the self or something terrible that might emerge from inside."

4

When you are not able to function to your fullest potential or ability, it is important to take a closer look at how and why you are feeling so much pressure. Anxiety comes in many forms. Sometimes, it is just a continuous, unpleasant sense of worry. It can also take the form of frightening, unexpected attacks called panic attacks. A panic attack can be one of the most terrifying things a person ever experiences.

Typical, everyday worry is not the same thing as an anxiety or panic attack, which is terrifying and debilitating, not merely unpleasant.

Bear in mind that anxiety and panic can be defeated. Therapy, medication, and learning new methods of breathing, positive thinking, and other techniques can provide hope for those who suffer and struggle with anxiety on a daily basis. No one can hope to go through life without ever feeling a bit of anxiety. But with knowledge and access to the right tools, we can all learn how to prevent anxiety and panic from controlling our lives. Normal worry and occasional nervousness and stress are normal parts of life, but you do not have to live with full-blown anxiety and panic attacks.

Why Do People Have Panic Attacks?

Nobody knows for sure why panic attacks happen. In the past, most experts thought of panic attacks as emotional problems. They believed that they happened because of complicated feelings that were bottled up inside a person. Today, most doctors agree that the attacks are caused as a result of environmental and neurological factors. For people who suffer from panic disorders, they usually show signs of below-average levels of serotonin, a type of neurotransmitter that plays a huge role in how well a person sleeps and his or her mood.

In some circumstances such as a life-threatening situation, these sensations are completely normal and healthy. When people are in danger, their bodies' natural defense mechanisms kick in. People are not even in control of these processes. They are instincts: natural, automatic reactions that help to ensure protection and survival.

When people are seriously threatened, something inside them

The adrenaline rush you get from dangerous situations is similar to the neurochemical rush that drives the fight-or-flight response.

urges them either to fight or run away in order to protect themselves from harm. This is called the fight-or-flight response. A person's mind receives a message of danger, and the body responds with the physical symptoms of panic. A panic attack happens when the mind and body seem to respond to danger when no danger is present. More recently, researchers have noted an addition to the fight-or-flight response. They call it a "freeze" response, and it occurs when someone's response to panic is to freeze like a deer in headlights. They can't fight or flee.

Panic attacks often happen for no reason, but some can be linked to a specific personal problem. The teen years are a very stressful time, full of new experiences that can create a buildup of tension. The pressure to do well in school is one. It is important to try your best in school because education is of great value throughout your life, but worrying about school to the point of severe anxiety can only do you harm. The only way to improve any situation in life is with a calm, focused mind.

Academic anxiety is a growing problem for teens in a time of ever-increasing expectations and competition.

A romantic breakup can be devastating to anyone, but young people tend to take the end of a relationship especially hard. Feelings of rejection, frustration, and loneliness can easily culminate in a panic attack. These same feelings can also occur when your parents fight or divorce. The death or illness of a parent is also a difficult thing to deal with, as are moving and changing schools. There are many other difficult situations teens must deal with, but the one thing they all seem to have in common is change. Everyone feels anxiety when adjusting to big changes in their lives. It is possible for any major life change to bring about one or more panic attacks, but keep in mind that over time, you'll eventually adjust to the new changes.

Symptoms of Panic Attacks

Panic attacks are characterized by many unpleasant symptoms. People may experience some of the following symptoms when they are having a panic attack:

- Feelings of warmth or coldness accompanied by sweating
- Racing heartbeat or heart pounding harder than normal
- Fear of losing control, dying, or going insane
- Feelings of mental confusion or disorientation
- Desire to run away or hide
- Difficulty breathing, including hyperventilating (breathing that is extremely shallow and fast), choking, tightness in the chest, and dry mouth

- Nausea and butterflies in the stomach
- Blurred vision, inability to focus eyes on one
  thing, sensation that things are being seen from
  a great distance or on a movie screen (some
  people describe this as a feeling of unreality
  because nothing seems as if it is really
  happening)
- Weakness, dizziness, and lightheadedness
- Uncontrollable shaking
- Muscle tension, soreness, and fatigue
- Tingling, numbness of the skin

The panic attack reaches a peak from about one to
ten minutes after it begins, then slowly decreases in
intensity. The duration of the entire attack can last any-
where from thirty minutes to several hours. Many people
suffering a panic attack for the first time end up being
rushed to a hospital emergency room. They think they are
having a heart attack because they feel their heart beating
so quickly.

There are many other medical conditions that can
cause sensations that feel like panic attacks. Some of
these conditions are hypoglycemia (low blood sugar),
complex partial seizures (a form of epilepsy), heart
arrhythmia (irregular heartbeat), and hyperventilation
syndrome (rapid breathing). Many prescription and even
over-the-counter drugs can produce side effects that feel
like panic attacks. A person who experiences panic attacks
should be carefully examined and diagnosed by a doctor,
just to be sure that he or she is not actually dealing with a
different or additional medical condition.

Stress can be a trigger to anxiety or panic attacks. Learning how to control your stress levels will also help you get panic and anxiety attacks under control.

The Negative Effects of Anxiety

There are many unpleasant physical symptoms that may accompany anxiety. Your heart may beat too fast or too hard. Headaches and body aches, cramps, coldness of the skin, and severe muscle tension can occur. And some people with severe anxiety may shake uncontrollably, feel butterflies in their stomachs, or have difficulty concentrating or sleeping. Negative moods and extreme irritability may cause a person with anxiety to lash out at people—family members, a boyfriend or girlfriend, a close friend, or someone who accidentally bumps into you in a crowded hallway at school.

The severity, or seriousness, of these possible symptoms will vary depending on the particular person and situation. A person who suffers from mild, occasional anxiety may experience the uncomfortable feelings described previously, but he or she will still be able to function normally. You may need to take time out to relax. A brisk walk or a long bath may help. Some people feel severe anxiety even when there are no particularly stressful incidents in their lives. A person who suffers from severe anxiety may get extremely upset over very small problems. People who have severe anxiety symptoms may become debilitated by them. This means that their high level of anxiety may cause them to have difficulty functioning. If you find it tough, tiresome, or scary to take part in your usual day-to-day activities, you should seek professional help.

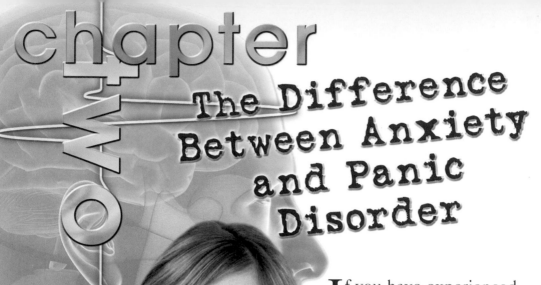

chapter two

The Difference Between Anxiety and Panic Disorder

If you have experienced a panic attack, it may be a great relief to learn that there is a name for the horrible combination of feelings that washed over you. It can also be comforting to realize that you are not the only one who has felt them before. Remember that there is nothing wrong with you because you have had, or continue to have, panic attacks. Many healthy individuals experience one or more panic attacks in their lifetime. It is estimated that within a year, a third of all Americans have at least one panic attack. People of all ages can have panic attacks. Studies show that more women suffer from these attacks than men.

There are many different kinds of anxiety disorders. The following are some common types.

Generalized Anxiety Disorder

Generalized anxiety disorder (GAD) is a serious anxiety problem. Someone with GAD feels afraid and worried all of the time, even when there is nothing to be afraid of or worried about. People with GAD tend to believe that some disaster is about to happen. Even if they realize that their constant worrying is not necessary or helpful, the fear does not go away. They can't relax. They may have trouble sleeping. People with GAD are unable to concentrate and are unable to focus enough to study for an exam. They'd worry about something happening to a relative who wasn't even sick. People suffering from GAD can always find something to worry about.

People with GAD may experience some or all of the common effects of anxiety, but much more intensely and more often than the average person. A GAD diagnosis is usually made if someone has suffered from anxiety for a majority of days over a period of six months, and if the anxiety interferes with his or her life. Those with mild cases of GAD may be able to function relatively easily in life, despite the disorder. But severe cases of GAD can prevent people from going about their day-to-day lives. If not properly treated, GAD may cause a person to be less happy or successful than if he or she was able to function at his or her fullest potential.

Severe generalized anxiety disorder may begin to affect your everyday life and prevent you from fully functioning. Even getting out of bed in the morning may become difficult.

Most people who have GAD begin to feel its effects as children or teens, but some may not even develop the disorder until they are adults. More women have GAD than men, and often many people in the same family have the disorder. Doctors believe that it is caused both by the chemical makeup of our brains and by the situations that occur in our lives. If you think that you may have GAD, you should speak with a counselor, a family member, or somebody else you trust. You should also see your doctor because some physical disorders such as an overactive thyroid (the thyroid regulates the metabolism) can cause the anxiety. With the proper treatment, many people with this problem learn to manage their worries and live successful and fulfilling lives.

Panic Disorder

Some people may experience only one panic attack in their lifetime, whereas others have them more often. So often, in fact, that they live in constant fear of the next attack. Repeat sufferers may be afraid to return to places where they have had panic attacks, or they may avoid certain social situations because they fear the embarrassment of being seen by others while having an attack. Some never leave their homes at all. Many doctors and psychiatrists would diagnose these people with a condition known as panic disorder.

     Panic disorder—frequent, uncontrollable panic attacks—resembles so many other medical conditions that its sufferers are often incorrectly diagnosed. The medical community is becoming much more educated about anxiety and panic, which makes it easier for people to find proper treatment for the disorder. It is more common than alcohol abuse or depression, and unfortunately, the majority of cases go untreated. As awareness about and information on panic disorders become more widespread, it's hoped that people with this disorder will seek help.

Worrying about worrying and being afraid of fear are major contributors to anxiety and panic attacks, creating a vicious circle.

Is It Anxiety or a Panic Disorder?

The question of whether a person suffers from generalized anxiety or a panic disorder is a tricky one and is best left to a professional diagnosis, since their symptoms are so similar. There are some basic differences, however.

If people feel anxiety frequently or all of the time, they may have GAD. If there are no panic attacks along with the anxiety, they probably do not have a panic dis-order. If both constant anxiety and panic attacks are present, the diagnosis will most likely be panic disorder.

People with GAD tend to worry about people's responses to them ("This school will never accept me," "What if my boss finds out how dumb I really am?"). Panic disorder sufferers are more concerned about losing control of their own bodies and minds ("I am going to have a heart attack," "What if I faint on the street?"). Panic disorder sufferers are also afraid of people's responses to their attacks, but that comes second to their fear of the attack itself.

16

chapter three

Common Anxiety Disorders

The term "anxiety disorder" is a broad one, encompassing many specific fears and anxieties, any of which can trigger a sudden, fleeting panic attack or more prolonged, gnawing, low-grade but debilitating anxiety. Some of the more common disorders will be discussed here.

Fear of Fear

Just thinking about a panic attack can sometimes bring one on. This is called anticipated or anticipatory anxiety, and it is a common trigger for a panic attack. Anticipated anxiety can also make people afraid of certain places or situations. Everybody associates places with feelings. For example, if you have a wonderful vacation in Hawaii, you will always have a positive image of Hawaii. If you were mugged on a certain street, going back to that street would probably make you pretty nervous. Although associating certain feelings with places is a normal thing to do, if the feelings are negative, giving in to them can keep people from doing things they enjoy.

Social Phobia

A common anxiety disorder among teens is social phobia (social anxiety disorder), the fear of being embarrassed by a social situation. The problem with being a teen is that social phobia is not exactly an unusual fear, and so unless it persists for six months and interferes with someone going to school, work, or out with his or her friends, doctors are reluctant to diagnose it. Sometimes, teens who develop social phobia were shy as children. It really is pretty normal to be self-conscious as a teen (bad skin days, bad hair days, getting changed for physical education when you've just put on some pounds). But people suffering from social anxiety disorder may blush, get the shakes, and feel nauseated when they have to answer a question in class, and they worry about it all the time. Or, they may be fine in class but terrified in the lunchroom.

Other phobias are of specific things or places. Snakes, elevators, tunnels, high places (or, more precisely, the edges of high places—few people are afraid of Denver), storms, or enclosed places are all fairly common ones.

Anxiety and panic attacks can make you feel isolated from your peers, especially if you feel embarrassed about your symptoms or worried about how people view you.

Post-Traumatic Stress Disorder

Some teens suffer from post-traumatic stress disorder (PTSD). This is the modern term for what, years ago, used to be called "shell shock." It was first diagnosed among WWI-era soldiers who had survived artillery shelling, bombardments, and trench warfare. Now doctors recognize that any traumatic situation that involved great physical harm or the threat of great physical harm can trigger it.

These high school girls from San Diego, California, comfort each other in the wake of a school shooting. The support of friends and loved ones can help prevent the occurrence of post-traumatic stress disorder.

When people find themselves in situations in which they feel helpless, fearful, horrified, or life-threatened, it can lead to this disorder. A teen who has been mugged, has been raped, or has experienced or witnessed great violence (for instance, the physical abuse of a parent or sibling) may suffer from flashbacks to this event. So may the survivor of a plane or car crash. He or she finds it impossible to feel that the event is truly in the past. Some people exhibit PTSD symptoms even when they were not directly involved in a traumatic situation, but they were there just as a witness.

Some common symptoms are nightmares or flashbacks of the event, avoidance of certain places or people that they associate with the event, emotional detachment from others, or jumpiness. When the symptoms of PTSD show varies. For some people, they exhibit symptoms soon after a traumatic event. In others, the signs might take a year. Or, a specific event such as an anniversary might trigger the symptoms. PTSD is diagnosed if symptoms of stress last longer than a month.

Obsessive-Compulsive Disorder

Obsessive-compulsive disorder (OCD) is another anxiety disorder—one that sometimes sounds funny, although not to the people who suffer from it. People with OCD are troubled by persistent, upsetting thoughts (obsessions). A common one is the fear of dirt or germs. They deal with this by developing rituals (compulsions) with which they try to control the fear. Someone who has OCD and suffers from the fear of contamination might wash his or her hands so many times a day that the hands become

Frequent and unnecessary hand-washing is a typical symptom of the anxiety disorder known as obsessive-compulsive disorder (OCD).

inflamed and even bloody, and yet the idea of stopping fills him or her with terror.

As with the other anxiety disorders, the difference between someone who is a little extra-careful about dirt (or especially worried about pesticides contaminating his or her food, for instance) and someone in need of help is a matter of severity. A disorder is something that interferes with ordinary life and causes great distress over a period of months.

Agoraphobia

Agoraphobia literally means "fear of the marketplace." Many people think of it as a fear of open spaces, or a fear of going outside of one's home. Actually, this phobia is much more complicated than that. What agoraphobics are afraid of is panic, and agoraphobia goes hand-in-hand with anxiety and panic attacks. In fact, the term "agoraphobia" is sometimes used interchangeably with "anticipatory anxiety."

Agoraphobia is a common anxiety disorder that often prevents its sufferers from leaving their houses or their "safe zones."

People with agoraphobia will avoid any place or situation that they associate with panicky feelings. Most agoraphobics have a "safe zone"—a place where they feel protected from anxiety and panic. Leaving the safe zone becomes a terrifying and painful thing to do.

Some agoraphobics suffer from recurring panic attacks, whereas others deal with anxious feelings without attacks. Agoraphobics may be too afraid to ever leave their homes. Others may struggle through jobs and busy social lives, always trying to hide the terror they feel inside.

MYTHS AND FACTS

Myth: You should be able to get over an anxiety or panic disorder by force of will.

Fact: Anxiety and panic disorders are real medical problems. Even though most people with anxiety and panic disorders know that their fears aren't rational, you can't just tell yourself that it's silly and make it go away. The only way it'll go away is with professional help.

Myth: A panic attack is dangerous because you might have a heart attack.

Fact: People suffering from a panic attack may feel as though they are going to die. It's a horrible feeling, but surviving panic disorder requires that people with anxiety understand that they are not in any immediate physical danger and that the feeling will pass.

Myth: Anxiety and panic disorders aren't real medical illnesses.

Fact: Yes, they are. Like many other illnesses they can be set off or worsened by things in your environment (intense pressure about college admissions, for instance) or in your psyche (a natural, inborn tendency to be a worrier). You can also have a biological tendency to be anxious.

chapter four

Getting Help

People who suffer from panic attacks and a panic disorder can easily feel stigmatized by others. Being stigmatized means being laughed at and made to feel excluded and disliked. Some people believe that panic attack sufferers are overreacting to something, imagining things, or just trying to get attention. They may not understand or believe that panic attacks and panic disorder are real. This is not fair.

Stigmatization may cause those who suffer from panic attacks to withdraw into a world of fear and depression. They may avoid trying to make friends because they feel ashamed of their problem. Also, a great many people who suffer from panic attacks and panic disorder must deal with employment difficulties, marital and other relationship problems, and reduced opportunities for travel.

Many turn to drugs or alcohol to numb their pain and anxiety. Around half the people who have a panic disorder will also have clinical depression at some time in their lives. However, the depression and substance abuse connected with panic disorder do not come only from external pressures. They also come from inside, from feeling powerless against constant attacks that come without warning. Additionally, the same brain chemistry that makes someone vulnerable to one anxiety disorder makes him or her vulnerable to others. Someone who is obsessive-compulsive can also develop an eating disorder. And the link between anxiety and depression is not only that having anxiety

Left untreated, anxiety and panic disorders can lead to depression, which, in turn, can increase your anxiety.

attacks is depressing. Someone who worries and feels pain about what is yet to come (anxiety) may also worry and grieve about the past (depression).

Sometimes, it is difficult to ask for help when you have anxiety and panic-related problems. You may feel too embarrassed to talk about what you're going through. You may be afraid that people will think you're crazy. Perhaps you feel you are going through a phase and the attacks will subside. Although you may be right, what if they keep happening? Or, what if the problem gets worse? There are many kinds of help available. It is important to remember that those who decide to fight have an excellent shot at victory and overcoming their anxiety.

Therapy and Support Groups

Therapy is something that may benefit many people, not just people who suffer from anxiety and panic. We all have problems. Speaking to a mental health professional can help us sort out the many difficult issues we face in our lives, including the shame and embarrassment that come with having a panic or anxiety disorder. To find a therapist, start with your family doctor or school counselor. He or she should be able to provide you with a list of respected professionals.

At your first appointment, be sure to ask the therapist about his or her experience with people who have anxiety and panic attacks. Do not be afraid to ask about his or her training and qualifications, as well as how frequently he or she would want to see you. Also try to find out about fees and sliding scale possibilities (a sliding scale is a pay scale

Sharing your feelings and concerns with a qualified therapist can help reduce your anxiety levels dramatically, even without the help of medication.

based on how much money you, or your parents, earn). Different professionals are likely to have different approaches to your treatment.

A psychiatrist is a medical doctor who can prescribe medications. He or she may also do therapy to discuss what you are feeling and what forces in your life, especially in the case of generalized anxiety disorder (GAD), may be contributing to your discomfort. Some therapists specialize in particular techniques. Other therapists, with experience in family counseling, may be most comfortable intervening if you need help dealing with demands that your family or school have placed on you.

It is very critical that you feel comfortable with your therapist. The two of you should click, and there is no way to force this to happen. Even the best therapist in the world is useless to a patient if there is no chemistry between them. It can take time for trust to develop, but you should feel that your therapist is someone to whom you can speak freely and honestly and without fear of judgment or disapproval.

A therapist can also put you in touch with others who share your problems, usually through a support group. A support group is exactly what it sounds like. It is a group of people who help each other out by offering support, compassion, and comfort. Support group members usually meet and discuss their problems under the guidance of a leader.

Cognitive-Behavioral Therapy

Cognitive-behavioral therapy (CBT) helps people with anxiety disorders change the way they think and act. You can work on combating negative thinking and a cognitive therapist can help. But a cognitive therapist will help you combat other thought patterns, encouraging you to learn to react differently to situations that cause anxiety or panic. Someone with a generalized anxiety disorder may have to identify and understand what he or she is anxious about, but he or she also needs to learn how to bear anxiety and to learn that it will go away. Someone with a panic disorder needs to learn that he or she does not have to go to the emergency room, that there is no danger of heart attack or other fatal risk.

Especially when people are afraid of something specific, be it a social situation or snakes, they can be helped to approach what they fear little by little, trusting the therapist to help them bear the anxiety that would otherwise make them flee. Running away reinforces the fear. It leaves you thinking, "OK, I got away this time!" But it does not make you less fearful in the future. People with anxiety and panic disorders often need help to realize that what they're

29

imagining is much worse than what will happen to them in real life.

Medications

There are many prescription medications available that help people who suffer from anxiety and panic attacks. The medications work to reduce different kinds of symptoms, and some may produce side effects. Remember that medications are there to help you overcome anxiety and panic, not to take away your problems. Ultimately, each of us is responsible for changing our own life. Prescription drugs can make the task a little easier.

If after consulting a doctor you do decide to start taking medication, you should be aware that some medications (particularly antidepressants) must be in your system for several weeks or longer before their effects can be felt. Your doctor will let you know when the prescribed medication should take effect. And always follow your doctor's dosage instructions carefully. Since everybody's mind and body is different, everybody reacts differently to medications. You could learn after trying a prescription drug that it is not really right for you, and your doctor may prescribe something different. Some trial and error may be necessary to find the medication that best suits you. Be sure to ask your doctor about possible side effects from medications and suggestions for relieving them.

How long do you stay on medication for anxiety and panic attacks? Again, this depends upon the doctor, the medication, and your reaction to it. It can take from three weeks to three months or more just to establish what your

In some cases, prescription antianxiety medication, when coupled with counseling or therapy, can help a person greatly reduce or even eliminate his or her anxiety symptoms and decrease the incidence of anxiety or panic attacks.

proper dosage should be. After that, you may stay on the medication permanently or for a year. However long you stay on the medicine, it is important to decrease your dosage gradually until you take nothing, rather than simply stopping suddenly.

Ten Great Questions to Ask Your Therapist

1. How do I know the difference between normal worries and the ones that need to be professionally treated?

2. How do I know what treatments are best for me?

3. If I have to take a medication, how long will it be until I know if it works? How long might I have to take it?

4. What are its possible side effects, and how can I treat them?

5. Is there an alternative to taking medication?

6. What should I do when I'm having a panic attack?

7. What can I do if I feel my parents and school are contributing to my anxiety through unreasonable demands and expectations?

8. How can I find out about support groups or counseling options?

9. What is your therapeutic approach to this type of problem?

10. How often will we meet? How long will we continue therapy?

chapter five

Living with Anxiety and Panic Attacks

There are many possible ways to deal with anxiety and panic, with or without medication. Maybe your anxiety or panic is not severe enough to warrant using prescription drugs. Or, maybe you would rather try some alternative solutions. Although there is nothing wrong with using medication to help overcome anxiety and panic, some people do prefer to rely on the natural healing powers of their minds and bodies.

Even if you do decide to use medication and therapy, both of which can be extremely helpful, keep in mind that they will not solve your problems like magic. Fighting anxiety and panic attacks is extremely hard work. One way or the other, treatment for anxiety and panic disorders involves changing how your brain works. This can be done directly, with drugs, or with therapy and other techniques. Often, a combination of treatments works best.

If, however, your anxiety or panic is causing you to miss school or work, or is otherwise having a serious impact on your daily life, you should also be talking to a doctor, therapist, or counselor, or be in a support group supervised by someone with mental health training. Real change means adopting new habits and ways of thinking in your daily life, and fighting to get rid of old, unhealthy habits. Here are some suggestions for doing just that.

Approaching your life and problems with a serene and positive attitude can help prevent stress from turning into anxiety.

Breathing

Some panic sufferers believe that learning how to breathe properly is the single most important key to overcoming a panic or anxiety attack. When we are calm, our breathing is slow and deep, and comes from the lower portion of our lungs. But when we panic, our breathing becomes fast and shallow, from the upper part of our lungs. This can cause other panic symptoms such as dizziness, nausea, and confusion. By learning to change the way you breathe, you can help control these symptoms when you feel an attack coming on. Calming your breath helps your heart rate to slow down, your blood pressure to decrease, your muscles to become less tense, and your entire body and mind to feel more relaxed.

To bring a proper amount of oxygen into your body, you need to breathe into your lower lungs. There is more room in your lower lungs than in your upper lungs, which allows for deeper breaths. Breathing this way is sometimes called abdominal breathing because filling up your lower lungs causes your abdomen (stomach) to stick out. When you take these deep breaths, your stomach should get bigger, then smaller, as you breathe in and out.

This is a good way to breathe all the time, not just during a panic attack. Learning the technique is simple. Just take in an amount of air that feels natural through your nose, and concentrate on bringing the air into your lower lungs. Put your hand on your abdomen. As you breathe in, it should be expanding. Release the air gently.

When you've mastered abdominal breathing, you can move on to calm breathing. This is breathing you do only when you feel panicky, and it helps you to feel more relaxed. Take a breath. Concentrate on keeping the breath long and slow. Fill your lower lungs, then the upper lungs. Now hold that breath and count to three. Exhale slowly through your mouth, with your lips partly closed (as if you're whistling). Focus on relaxing your entire body as you exhale.

You should try to practice this about ten times a day for a few weeks so that you are prepared to do it when feelings of panic strike. It can be a great break from homework or an excellent way to relax before going to bed.

Here is an even more powerful way to do calm breathing. It takes a little longer and requires more concentration, but it can help to give you even more control over panicky thoughts. Take a slow, deep abdominal breath, and as you exhale quietly say the word "relax." Now close your eyes. Take ten deep but natural breaths and count down out loud with each exhale. Start with "ten" and work your way down to "one." As you do this, scan your body for signs of tension. If you notice tense areas, let them loosen. Do not open your eyes again until you reach "one."

Meditation is a proven technique for reducing stress and increasing a sense of peace, security, and well-being.

Meditation

Meditation is an even deeper kind of relaxation. People who learn to meditate report incredible benefits in their lives, from better physical health to spiritual insights and revelations. Yoga, an Eastern tradition that involves deep relaxation and holding the body in specially developed positions (kind of like stretching), has also been shown to bring about these benefits.

Yoga and meditation can be excellent tools in fighting panic. They can help panic sufferers to find balance and calmness, and help to bring the body and mind together in a healing way. If you think you may be interested in studying these disciplines, check your Yellow Pages for schools in your area (look under "Yoga," "Meditation," or "Spirituality").

Positive Thinking

Approaching your life and your problems in a positive way is essential in fighting anxiety and panic. In a way, a panic attack is like a collection of negative thoughts that runs out of control. If you can gain control over your thoughts, you can fight panic more effectively. You have to be able to tell yourself that you can do it.

Pay close attention to your thoughts through-out your day. How often

With some hard work and professional help, you can set yourself free from anxiety and panic attacks.

do you tell yourself, "I'm hopeless," "I can't handle this," or "My life is going nowhere"? You need to block these negative, self-critical thoughts. Criticizing yourself will get you nowhere. It only makes you feel worse, and bringing about positive change becomes more and more difficult. Any time you notice that you are beating yourself up or feeling hopeless, tell yourself to stop. Stop right where you are and fight these negative thoughts with positive ones. Say out loud: "I can do this. I am capable. I am strong enough to deal with this." Be confident. Compliment yourself, and believe it.

Setting and Approaching Your Goals

The goal of freedom from panic may seem difficult to reach. After suffering from uncontrollable anxiety and panic attacks, a person can become discouraged. Conquering these problems sometimes takes a long time and requires a great deal of struggle. So, how does a panic sufferer work toward an end to the pain without losing hope?

The best way to go is one small step at a time. You need to set both long-term and short-term goals. Long-term goals are the big ones. These are the ultimate things you want to accomplish in fighting your problem. But since these goals are so big, you need to create a series of smaller steps in order to get to them. Think of short-term goals as steps on the ladder to success. Each long-term goal has its own series of short-term goals. For example, a long-term goal may be going out with friends and enjoying yourself without having a panic attack. Then decide which of these goals will be the most difficult to accomplish.

Now you will set short-term goals to lead you to your long-term goals. Start with one of the least difficult long-term goals to accomplish. Then try to come up with some small step to take that will bring you closer to that goal. For example, let's say your goal is to eat in your favorite restaurant without having a panic attack. A good small step may be walking near the restaurant. Stand across the street from it, and try to control any fear that arises.

After one small step is conquered, more ideas for other short-term goals will probably come to you. Perhaps the next step could be standing closer to the restaurant or looking into the window. These goals seem much easier and more possible to achieve than the long-term ones, yet they do take you closer to what you ultimately want to achieve.

Be patient. Be as kind to yourself as you can. Ask for help. There is no quick fix in fighting anxiety and panic, but you will be surprised at how good you feel when you are working productively toward the goal of feeling better. Before you know it, you'll be well on your way to feeling happy, healthy, and peaceful.

abdominal breathing Method of deep breathing that expands the abdomen (stomach) and aids in relaxation.

agoraphobia Irrational fear or panic associated with particular places and situations.

anticipatory anxiety Anxiety that is brought on by anticipating a panic attack, usually because of an associated place or situation.

anxiety Fear, worry, or dread.

calm breathing A kind of deep breathing that can help to prevent a panic attack.

debilitated Prevented from functioning in society or from working toward a desired goal.

fight-or-flight response Instinct brought about by a threatening situation that motivates people either to run away or fight in order to protect themselves.

generalized anxiety disorder (GAD) Disorder characterized by constant feelings of worry.

instincts Automatic reactions that help to ensure our protection and survival.

irrational fear Fear that occurs even when a situation does not call for it; inappropriate, unprovoked anxiety.

lower lungs Area of the lungs with the most room for air; best to use for deep breathing.

meditation Means of focusing and disciplining the mind through deep relaxation and concentration.

panic attack Collection of negative, frightening thoughts and feelings that becomes out of control.

panic disorder Disorder characterized by frequent panic attacks.

safe zone Area where an agoraphobic feels safe and protected from anxiety and panic.

stigmatized Made to feel laughed at, excluded, or disliked.

triggers People, places, and situations that can bring on a panic attack.

yoga Means of focusing and disciplining the mind through deep relaxation, concentration, and holding the body in specially designed poses.

American Institute of Stress
124 Park Avenue
Yonkers, NY 10703
(914) 963-1200
Web site: http://www.stress.org
This nonprofit organization provides a clearinghouse of information on stress and ways to deal with it.

American Psychological Association (APA)
750 First Street NE
Washington, DC 20002-4242
(800) 374-2721
Web site: http://www.apa.org
The APA is a scientific and professional organization that represents psychology in the United States. With 148,000 members, the APA is the largest association of psychologists worldwide.

Anxiety Disorders Association of America
8730 Georgia Avenue, Suite 600
Silver Spring, MD 20910
(240) 485-1001
Web site: http://www.adaa.org
This nonprofit organization seeks to prevent, treat, and cure anxiety disorders and provide education on anxiety-related issues.

Mental Health America
2000 N. Beauregard Street, 6th Floor
Alexandria, VA 22311
(800) 969-6642
TTY: (800) 433-5959

Web site: http://www.nmha.org
This is the country's largest nonprofit organization that works on all aspects of mental health.

National Alliance on Mental Illness
2107 Wilson Boulevard, Suite 300
Arlington, VA 22201-3042
(888) 999-6264
Web site: http://www.nami.org
This national organization aims to provide support, advocacy, and education on mental health issues.

National Institute of Mental Health (NIMH)
6001 Executive Boulevard, Room 8184, MSC 9663
Bethesda, MD 20892-9663
(866) 615-6464 (toll-free)
Web site: http://www.nimh.nih.gov
NIMH supports innovative science that will transform the diagnosis, treatment, and prevention of mental disorders, paving the way for a cure. The NIMH's mission is to reduce the burden of mental illness and behavioral disorders through research on mind, brain, and behavior.

Hotlines

Covenant House Hotline
(800) 999-9999
This is a twenty-four-hour information and crisis hotline for youth, teens, and parents staffed by crisis counselors. It gives callers locally based referrals throughout the United States and provides help for youth and parents regarding drugs, abuse, homelessness, runaway children, and message relays.

National Referral Network for Kids in Crisis
(800) 543-7283
This service is available twenty-four hours a day, seven days a week, for professionals, parents, and adolescents.

National Youth Crisis Hotline
(800) HIT-HOME (448-4663)
This hotline provides counseling and referrals to local drug treatment centers, shelters, and counseling services. It responds to youth dealing with pregnancy, molestation, suicide, and child abuse, and operates twenty-four hours, seven days a week.

Web Sites

Due to the changing nature of Internet links, Rosen Publishing has developed an online list of Web sites related to the subject of this book. This site is updated regularly. Please use this link to access the list:

http://www.rosenlinks.com/tmh/aapa

Anxiety/Panic Attack Resource Site. "Anxiety and Panic Attacks."Retrieved February 2008 (http://www.anxietypanic.com).

Barlow, David H. *Anxiety and Its Disorders: The Nature and Treatment of Anxiety and Panic*. New York, NY: The Guilford Press, 2004.

Berzoff, Joan, Laura Melano Flanagan, and Patricia Hertz. *Inside Out and Outside In: Psychodynamic Clinical Theory and Practice in Contemporary Multicultural Contexts*. Northvale, NJ: Jason Aronson, 2007.

Bourne, Edmund J. *Anxiety and Phobia Workbook*. Oakland, CA: New Harbinger Publications, 2005.

Bourne, Edmund J, and Lorna Garano. *Coping with Anxiety, Fear, and Worry*. Oakland, CA: New Harbinger Publications, 2003.

Buell, Linda Manassee. *Panic and Anxiety Disorder: 121 Tips, Real-Life Advice, Resources, and More*. 2nd ed. Poway, CA: Simply Life, 2003.

Burns, David D., M.D. *When Panic Attacks: The New, Drug-Free Anxiety Therapy That Can Change Your Life*. New York, NY: Broadway, 2007.

Christ, James J. *What to Do When You're Scared and Worried: A Guide for Kids*. Minneapolis, MN: Free Spirit, 2004.

Clark, Carolyn Chambers. *Living Well with Anxiety: What Your Doctor Doesn't Tell You . . . That You Need to Know*. New York, NY: Collins, 2006.

Connolly, Sucheta, Cynthia L. Petty, and David A. Simpson. *Anxiety Disorders*. New York, NY: Chelsea House, 2006.

Foa, Edna B., and Linda Wasmer Andrews. *If Your Adolescent Has an Anxiety Disorder: An Essential*

Resource for Parents. New York, NY: Oxford
    University Press, 2006.
Medicinenet. "Panic Attacks (Panic Disorders)." 2007.
    Retrieved February 2008 (http://www.medicinenet.
    com/panic_disorder/article.htm).
Morris, Tracy L., and John S. March, eds. *Anxiety Disorders
    in Children and Adolescents*. 2nd ed. New York, NY:
    The Guilford Press, 2004.
National Mental Health Information Center. "Anxiety
    Disorders."Retrieved February 2008 (http://
    mentalhealth.samhsa.gov/publications/allpubs/
    ken98-0045/default.asp).
Rosen, Marvin. *The Effects of Stress and Anxiety on the Family*.
    New York, NY: Chelsea House, 2002.
Rutledge, Jill Zimmerman. *Dealing with the Stuff That
    Makes Life Tough: The Ten Things That Stress Teen Girls
    Out and How to Cope with Them*. New York, NY:
    McGraw Hill, 2003.
Seaward, Brian, and Linda Bartlett. *Hot Stones and Funny
    Bones: Teens Helping Teens Cope with Stress and Anger*.
    Deerfield Beach, FL: HCI Teens, 2002.
Sluke, Sara Jane, and Vanessa Torres. *The Complete Idiot's
    Guide to Dealing with Stress for Teens*. New York, NY:
    Alpha, 2001.
Spencer, Elizabeth DuPont, Robert L. DuPont, and
    Caroline M. DuPont. *The Anxiety Cure for Kids: A
    Guide for Parents*. Hoboken, NJ: Wiley, 2003.
Van Duyne, Sara. *Stress and Anxiety-Related Disorders*.
    Berkeley Heights, NJ: Enslow Publishers, 2003.

About the Author

Judith N. Levin is an author and librarian with a variety of science, health, and wellness titles to her credit, including books on depression and mood disorders, self-image, and diabetes.

Photo Credits

Cover, p. 1 (top left) © www.istockphoto.com/Petro Feketa; cover, p. 1 (middle left) © www.istockphoto.com/Dawna Stafford; cover, p. 1 (bottom left) © www.istockphoto.com/Eric Simard; cover (foreground) © www.istockphoto.com/Jim Jurica; cover, pp. 1, 3 (head and brain) © www.istockphoto.com/Vasiliy Yakobchuk; p. 3 (laptop) © www.istockphoto.com/Brendon De Suza; pp. 3, 4, 12, 17, 25, 33 (books) © www.istockphoto.com/Michal Koziarski; pp. 4, 12, 17, 25, 33 (head) © www.istockphoto.com; p. 4 © www.istockphoto.com/Nicholas Monu; p. 5 © John Birdsall/The Image Works; pp. 6, 16, 22 Shutterstock.com; p. 7 © www.istockphoto.com/Eric Hood; p. 10 © AJPhoto/Photo Researchers, Inc.; p. 12 © www.istockphoto.com/Jason Lugo; p. 14 © Scientifica/Visuals Unlimited; p. 17 © www.istockphoto.com/Quavondo Nguyen; p. 19 © Bob Daemmrich/The Image Works; p. 20 Tom Kurtz/AFP/Getty Images; p. 23 Tara Moore/Stone/Getty Images; p. 25 © www.istockphoto.com/Tracy Whiteside; p. 26 © www.istockphoto.com/Andrea Gingerich; p. 28 © Burger/Photo Researchers, Inc.; p. 31 © Ellen Senisi/The Image Works; p. 33 © www.istockphoto.com/4x6; p. 34 © www.istockphoto.com/Agata Malchrowicz; p. 36 © AP Images; p. 37 © www.istockphoto.com/Ryan KC Wong.

Designer: Nelson Sá
Photo Researcher: Cindy Reiman